I Got Something to Say!

The Book in Me

Valerie Devone-Grimes

Copyright © 2025 I Got Something to Say! The Book in Me

For information regarding permission, write to
Email: valscraftcity@aol.com

Follow us on Facebook: http://www.facebook.com/pages/eatnenjoy

For information regarding permission, write to
135-05 Foch Blvd, South Ozone Park, NY 11420
Attention Mrs. Valerie Devone-Grimes

Credits: www.biblegateway.com

Paperback ISBN:978-1-965757-41-3

Printed in the USA.

Dedication:

We have dedicated this writing guide to my Lord and Savior Jesus Christ.

I also dedicate this book to my parents,

David and Marjorie Devone

To every aspiring writer that has no idea of what to write or how to start, I wrote this book with you in mind. It is designed to help you navigate through your writing assignment. I pray that you will apply this wisdom learned to your writing process to help you along the way.

I pray that "I Got Something to Say! The Book in Me" has been a blessing to you and your writing journey.

Table of Contents:

Bio:

Valerie Devone-Grimes is a multi-talented woman who excels in crafting, jewelry-making, cooking, baking, and poetry. She spreads joy through her various pursuits and has been successful in decorating cakes where she has been given the nickname "The Cake Lady," and has appeared on the QPTV show sharing her knowledge of cooking and baking. Valerie has been the owner of a variety store for several years called Val's Dollar Spot. She is also a designer of wedding accessories.

Valerie has also taught cooking, poetry classes, and worked with children daycare centers and public libraries. She also worked at a nursing home for twenty-six years and is now active in her community. Valerie also has been a vendor of a variety of goods in her local church community for five years in St. Albans Queens, NY.

She is married to Rodney Grimes and from their union have a son named Isaiah. Family is the driving force in Valerie's life. Now, she shares her heartfelt love for writing with the world. Valerie has written and published fifty-two books and counting.

Stay connected with us on social media:

Facebook: Visit Valerie Stories page for updates on my latest books and behind-the-scenes content.

Instagram: Follow our Eatnenjoy21 page for a glimpse into our creative process and sneak peeks of upcoming releases.

I Got Something to Say!
The Book in Me

Valerie Devone-Grimes

Introduction:

You've decided to write a book. Congratulations. Deciding what you want to write is the first step to publication. I want to welcome you to my book *"I Got Something to Say! The Book in Me "*. In this book we will deal with overcoming the writer's block, motivation, and heart of the author. Writing a book requires you to practice writing every day or as often as you can.

Whether you are writing poems, memoirs, or novels. You must put time and love into everything that you do. Enjoy the test in the beginning of the book and practice words we use in our everyday vocabulary. This may start showing you some weaknesses and strengths you have in writing.

In the book *"I Got Something to Say! The Book in Me"* is design for those interested in writing a book or learning about the writing and publishing process. Everyone's process is not the same. You will learn the fundamentals of writing, basic skills, and techniques for getting started.

Our motto is "There is nothing to it, but to do it!" I pray that each person that starts your writing journey will take on the mindset of, "I can do anything". It is biblically based, and taken from Philippians 4:13, *"I can do all things through Christ that strengthens me." (NKJV).*

Section #1
The Writer's Jumpstart

Thirteen Spelling, Punctuation & Grammar Checklist:

1) **Spelling** - Check for misspelled words.

2) **Misused Words** - Review a running list of words you're prone to misuse (even if they are typos).

3) **Commas** - Review for comma splices (a comma joining two independent clauses without the presence of a coordinating conjunction) as well revise commas used in a series.

4) **Apostrophes** - Look for all non-possessive plural nouns (ensure there is no apostrophe) as well review contractions or possessive nouns for apostrophe.

5) **Colons and Semicolons** - Check colons for introducing long quotes, announcements and introducing a series without expression such as namely, that is etc. Fix comma splices by joining independent clauses with a semicolon when stylistically correct.

6) **Dashes and Hyphens** - Ensure dashes are not excessively used and they maintain a space on either side. Check whether your compound modifiers are using hyphens correctly (no space on either side).

7) **Run-on Sentences** -Find every occurrence of coordinating conjunctions-and, but, or, and yet-and revise any run-on sentences.

8) **Other Punctuation** - Review for excessive exclamation points and ellipses as well as period usage relative to quotation marks.

9) **Sentence Structure - 4 main types of Sentences:**
You will not become a better writer simply by learning to name the several types of sentences, but you will develop a more sophisticated understanding of how language works. If you would like to make certain that you understand how to identify.

10) **Simple sentence:** A simple sentence contains only one independent clause. An independent clause is a group of words. (With a subject and a verb) that expresses a complete thought.

11) **Compound sentences:** A compound sentence contains at least two independent clauses. These clauses are joined by a coordinating conjunction or a semicolon. A coordinating conjunction is a word those glues words, phrases or clauses together.

12) **Complex sentences:** A complex sentence contains a subordinate clause and an independent clause. A subordinate clause is a group of words that have a subject and a verb but does not express a complete thought.

13) **Compound Complex sentences:** A compound-complex sentence contains at least two independent clauses and at least one subordinate clause.

Number 9 is a reminder to pay attention to what you are always writing about and for. This book that you embark on writing will follow you for the rest of your life. You must make this count.

<u>Overcoming Writer's Block</u>:

What is writer's block all about?

Writer's block is about the author experiencing a sense of fear that they may not be able to finish the task of writing a book. So, when it comes time to put pen to paper, they experience a mental block, unable to find words to write, which can last minutes, hours, days and or weeks, if not years.

Writer's block can be destructive to any author by causing them to give up trying to write a book. It will also cause one to write and produce less than what they're used to producing. Writer's block can be common among the best of writer's and unpredictable.

<u>Some potential causes</u>: stress, trauma, a loss of a loved one, loss of a job, depression, anxiety, lack of confidence, doubt, high expectations, unreasonable expectations, unpreparedness, lack of enthusiasm, self-criticism, criticism, etc.

<u>Some possible solutions:</u> Personal affirmation spoken to build confidence, pray and give thanks to God, reading and exploring other books, love who you are, be kind to yourself, change of environment, change of routine, exercise, embrace and own your call to writing, and consider your audience, etc.

<u>Some Solution Prompts:</u>

1) **Get organized!** Keep all your stories, photos, and other pieces of inspiration in a central location.

2) **Keep notebooks:** Keep a selection of notebooks handy in a variety of locations for instant inspiration. When an idea strikes, write it down immediately. Remember to glance through these ideas when you need some inspiration.

3) **Free-Writing journal:** Set a time limit or page limit and write continuously without stopping until your goal has been reached. Write down everything that comes to mind, random and unimportant as it may seem.

4) **Record your ideas on a voice recorder:**
Using a smart device, record your story ideas that unexpectedly come when paper and pencils are not available. Revisit audio later or as soon as possible.

5) **Pick up a pen:** If you have been typing away endlessly at your keyboard to no avail, pick up a pen. Try longhand or reach for a pencil. Nothing beats the feeling of a free-flowing lead gripped tightly between your fingers.

6) **Start with the easiest part:** You are not limited to starting with an introduction, try starting in the middle or with the conclusion of the story. Fill in all the blanks later.

7) **Reduce noise distractions:** Ringing or vibrating cell phones can quickly break your train of thought; leave these in another room until you are finished. Avoid loud music and sudden vocal distractions or opt for a pair of earplugs if you are unable to do so.

8) **Work on an outline, summary, or table of contents:** If you are unable to find the perfect words, consider simply working on the outline or a table of contents.

9) **Reference books:** Remember there's value in a good old-fashioned book. Flip through some reference material and seeing physical words in print often provides inspiration. Keep a thesaurus, concise dictionary, and English resources close at hand and see what turns up.

10) **Use a bulletin board.** Hang a bulletin board in a strategic place; keep posting anything that provides inspiration, lists of words that you often misspell, photographs, inspirational quotes, and words of encouragement, vision board, and or new articles.

11) **Protection for book content:** If you are not yet ready to share ideas with a friend, blabber non-stop into Dictaphone or voice recorder.

I hope you found some valuable information within this writer's guide that can help you with overcoming writer's block.

Finding Time to Write:

I wrote every time that I had a chance; I wrote in places people don't normally do instead of talking on the job I kept writing. I wrote when I was in the bathroom sitting on the toilet, waking up out of my sleep at 3 am and sitting on the side of bed and still writing. Even when I am driving, I must pull over to write. When on a long line in the stores and when I go to bookstores; I would sit on the floor and write. Even when I went to church, I would write during services. You see when you are true to your craft of writing it will open your mind to so many possibilities in every area of your life.

Write in the freedom of your spirit, body and soul never take no for an answer. You can do whatever God has placed down inside of you. Pour out your energy through the ability of your writing skills deep down inside of you. Evaluate yourself to the next level in finishing and coming to full completion of a project in your life. See, make up your mind you will devote yourself to this task before you. The stories, articles, recipes, and romance stories knocking at door waiting to be unleashed into a book.

People may laugh when you say I want to write a book that they think is not possible. Speak that back to this person and ask them, "When was the last time you wrote a bestseller that was in Sunday paper? Don't let anyone knock you down, get back up. See you need to keep that notebook and pen by your side until your task is finished. The storyteller if that you who you believe in yourself every day and don't doubt yourself for one moment.

Here are some ideas to help you find time to write, turn off your phones, reduce or cut down on TV viewing time, time yourself when writing or schedule it. Now you should always try to carry a notebook or laptop to cafes to write, have a notebook and always pen handy or bring a handheld tape recorder with you in your bag.

<u>Motivation:</u>

Before writing anything, we need to pray about what we want to write. Then allow the Lord to give us direction in sharing what it is we are writing for the world.

The moment an idea runs through your mind it is time to start writing down those thoughts and ideas on paper. As the river of information flows through your brain; take a deep breath and push through until the moment finishes.

<u>*Say it Loud, Say it Proud and Say It Right!*</u>

Speak out the paragraphs and allow the pages to be born out of the book that is within you.

We all get inspired by pictures, reading a book, movie or just by thought so it is to allow your wings to fly high in the sky as they can go.

Make it a habit to write every day or as often as you can, along with reading every day. I'm not saying I'm writing a new story every night. I'm telling you to write something every day. By making writing an everyday habit, you will be less likely to stop, thus establishing one of the cures for writer's block.

But you need to plan about when and where you will write. Here are some ideas.

- o   *Organize working 4 days a week and use the fifth for writing.*
- o   *Get up an hour earlier and write before the household gets up.*
- o   *Take lunch hour at work several times a week, find a room and write then.*
- o   *On weekends when I am not doing household chores. I will get a cleaner to do the household cleaning and use that time to write.*
- o   *On the commute (train, bus)*
- o   *Hanging out on my day off at a café or writing lounge*
- o   *Talking to people might inspire the subject of your next piece.*
- o   *Exercise positively affects the levels of certain mood-enhancing neurotransmitters in the brain.*
- o   *Write down random ideas, sentences or thoughts that work.*
- o   *Call an old friend.*
- o   *Read some inspiring quotes to get you started.*
- o   *Listen to music (try classical or jazz to mix it up).*

Life is all about choices. You get to choose. You get to decide how you spend your free time. But many writers forget that writing is a choice. Finding time to write when you are already busy as hell may seem like a huge challenge.   It may even feel impossible at times. But here is a little secret that may help put things into perspective: It is not about finding time to write; it's about making time to write.

Some Questions to Ask Yourself:

1. Why do I want to become an author?

    _____

    _____

2. What message do you want to convey to the world?

    _____

    _____

3. What type of book are you considering writing?

    _____

    _____

4. Who is your target audience?

    _____

    _____

5. What or Who has inspired you to start writing?

    _____

    _____

6. What level of commitment are you willing to make towards writing?

    _____

    _____

7. Are you interested in traditional or self-publishing?

    _____

    _____

8. Are you open to joining a writer's group?

_____

_____

9. Do you have a designated place to write? Where is it?

_____

_____

_____

_____

10. What is the most difficult part for you about writing?

_____

_____

11. What genre will you focus on your writing? (Art, drama, supernatural, thriller, or suspense)?

_____

_____

12. When did you first realize that you wanted to become an author?

_____

_____

13. What is your favorite part about the writing process?

_____

_____

14. Are you familiar with writer's block and what does it mean?

_____

_____

15. Are you familiar with copyright and its laws?

_____

_____

16. Why is it important to save your manuscript(s) in more than one place? (Computer, thumb, or flash drive)?

_____

_____

17. Do you know what ISBNs are and what they mean for writing a book? Write your thoughts.

_____

_____

18. Are you willing to invest in writing materials to help further your writing journey?

_____

_____

19. How do you feel about supporting other authors?

_____

_____

20. Are you expecting to make a living writing book?

_____

_____

<u>Essential Writing Vitamins:</u>

<u>Definition:</u>

The summary should include the most important plot points and characters. Your summary should get the main point of the book across to someone who has never read the actual book.

A-ACTION Start with you: On a film set, they shout the word "ACTION!" Without it, there's no indication for the actors, videographers, and other essential personnel to do their jobs. Use this same principle to get fired up, focused and compelled to write.

B-BELIEVE in Yourself: That small voice in your head your inner critic wants you to second guess yourself. It wants you to stop trying and give up. Tell it to shut up. Focus on the remarkable value you offer because if you believe in yourself, the world will too.

C-CREATIVITY is Limitless: Expand your creativity and give your audience something they haven't seen before by creating something truly remarkable. Challenge yourself to take a different direction and add a spark to your usual routine.

D-DISTRACTIONS Kill Your Writing: Temptation is all around us. Sure, it can be fun to check emails, play games or chat with friends when you really should be hard at work, but it doesn't get the job done. Challenge yourself to start and finish a project while squashing temptation.

E-EXERCISE Daily: Create your own exercises to tap into your creativity and sharpen your skills by making writing a daily habit. You don't want to lose your edge, so create a writing routine to stay on top of your writing.

F-FEAR is Not Real: In Proverbs 23:7 "As a man thinketh in his heart, so is he" This is a spiritual principle which can never be broken; it always works, much like the law of sowing and reaping. Let your fears go.

G-GOALS Map Success: Create a goal road map. Tracking goals will show you how far you've come, your next milestone and help you stay on course. Motivate yourself to make new goals and complete them routinely.

H-HONESTY Wins: If you paint an authentic picture based on honesty, your audience will learn to trust you as a credible source. It's not necessary to intimidate or go over your audience's head with jargon; rather simply build on the connections you make and stay true to your word.

I-INFLUENCE Others: Writing isn't simply about communicating a message. It's about engagement and influence. Ensure your writing is clear and concise, so your influence impacts a wider audience.

J-JOURNAL to Innovate: Journaling can help you generate ideas, develop better writing habits, enhance your skill set and create a personal archive for "aha!" moments throughout your day. Start journaling as a part of your daily routine.

K-Know Your Audience: It's easier now than ever before to be data driven, track clicks, views, purchases, and other trends to stay on top of your audience. Research what information your readers are searching, ask questions and experiment.

L-LEARN to LAUGH: You don't always have to be so serious; tickle someone's funny bone and lighten the mood! Laughter is a great medicine and can be used to show your audience to another side.

M-MASTER Your Technique: Use any quality-driven tools necessary to become an expert in your field. By taking massive action, setting goals, writing daily and learning about your audience, your focus will be stronger than ever before.

N-NETWORK to Build Connections: Join relevant groups, attend or create events and don't just talk, listen. Being a good listener will help you keep a pulse on trends in your niche and where you can innovate to create value.

O-ORGANIZE Your Writing: Deliver an impact by solidifying your structure before you write. Develop a clear outline, whether it's an article's format or a whole series of articles so you're creating value, not derivative content.

P-PERFECT you're PROFILE: Your Expert Author Profile showcases your skills and experience, your top websites and social media. Use your real name and display a professional picture of yourself to increase transparency and credibility.

Q-Quality is Top Priority: Quality is the standard of something as measured against other things of a similar kind. Don't cheapen your niche or disappoint readers. Write quality content that stands out.

R- Read Regularly: Find the time to read to stay on top of the latest trends, improve your writing skills and increase your writing, reading endurance.

S-Stress Reduction: Stress can lead to illness, causes procrastination and it can decrease the quality of your writing. Manage stress by identifying the signs beforehand and creating a stress management plan.

T-TIME to Manage Writing: Time management is difficult. Be realistic, inform others of your writing schedule, avoid distractions, change your own rules for more effective strategies and take your writing seriously.

U-UNDERSTAND Your Role: Do you consider yourself an author or are you writing a casual affair? Authors are informative leaders who provide valuable, quality content that benefits readers. Casual writers write for themselves. Take a closer look into the value you're offering and adjust accordingly to fulfill your role.

V-VICTORIES can be BIG or Small: Small victories are a great way to take charge of your life and lend a positive sense of direction. Start small, focus on the path to completion and celebrate when it's time.

W-WISDOM: Knowledge is important, but readers often seek wisdom in what to write on every project.

X-XEROGRAPHY: We know one of the last processes to print your book. an electrostatic printing process for copying text or graphics whereby areas on a sheet of paper corresponding to the **image** areas of the original are sensitized with a charge of **static electricity** so that, when powdered with a toner carrying an opposite charge, only the charged areas retain the toner, **which** is then fused to the paper to make it permanent. (Printing, Lithography & Bookbinding)

Y-YOU: This is a day for a fresh start to become the writer you are. The number one goal is for you to fall in love with what you write. Take the time to speak from the heart with understanding and wisdom and bring someone into your story and speak to them. If this, you keep pens handy with a pad to convey your message to the people.

Z-ZINES: A zine is most commonly a small circulation self-published work of original writers. This is done by non-professional writers. They have stories or series about different subjects that interest people on all levels.

Section #2
Writing Mechanics & Style

Grammar Check:

Now before we get into the book here is a little test to see where you are in your grammar:

1. Which of the following spellings is correct?

    a) acomodate

    b) accomodate

    c) acommodate

    d) accommodate

    e) Don't Know

2. Which of the following spellings is preferred in US English?

    a) acknowledgment

    b) acknowledgement

    c) acknowlegment

    d) acknowlegement

    e) Don't Know

3. Which of the following spellings is correct?

a) arguement

b) argument

c) arguemant

d) arguemint

e) Don't Know

4. Which of the following spellings is correct?

a) comitment

b) comitmment

c) commitment

d) comitmant

e) Don't Know

5. Which of the following spellings is correct?

a) consensus

b) concensus

c) consencus

d) consenssus

e) Don't Know

6. Which of the following spellings is correct?

a) deductible

b) deductable

c) deductuble

d) deductabel

e) Don't Know

7. Which of the following spellings is always preferred in US English and preferred as an adjective in British English? ("He has insulin-_____ diabetes.")

a) dependant

b) depindant

c) dependent

d) dependunt

e) Don't Know

8. Which of the following spellings is correct?

a) embarras

b) embaras

c) embarass

d) embarrass

e) Don't Know

9. Which of the following spellings is correct?

a) existance

b) existence

c) existanse

d) existanc

e) Don't Know

10. Which of the following spellings is correct for a page at the beginning of a book?

a) foreward

b) forword

c) forworde

d) foreword

e) Don't Know

11. Which of the following spellings is correct?

a) harass

b) haras

c) harrass

d) herrass

e) Don't Know

12. Which of the following spellings is correct?

a) inadvertant

b) inadvartant

c) inadvartent

d) inadvertent

e) Don't Know

13. Which of the following spellings is correct?

a) indispensabel

b) indispensible

c) indispensable

d) indespensible

e) Don't Know

14. Which of the following spellings is preferred in American English?

a) judgement

b) judgment

c) judgemant

d) judgmant

e) Don't Know

15. Which of the following spellings is correct?

a) liason

b) liasson

c) liasone

d) liaison

e) Don't Know

You have now finished the test!

<u>Answer Key:</u>

1-D. accommodate   14- A. judgement
2-B. acknowledges   15- B. liaison
3-B. argument
4-C. commitment
5- A. consensus
6-A. deductible
7-C. dependent
8-D. embarrass
9-B. existence
10-D. foreword
11-D. harasses
12-D. inadvertent
13- C. indispensable

Knowing the Heart of Author:

Every single person is a writer, truly! Each one of us carries within us a universe of stories, tales of life, adventures, and encounters that demand to be shared. What would your story be if you dared to spill it straight from the depths of your soul? In Psalm 45:1(NIRV)"*My heart is full of beautiful words as I say my poem for the king. My tongue is like the pen of a skillful writer.*" Creative words for writing always pique interest.

Now is the moment to dive headfirst into your dream of becoming an author who crafts your own stories with fiery passion. When you allow yourself as an author to immerse yourself in the art of storytelling, it's a powerful gift that you can unleash upon people across the globe. What burning subject or riveting topic do you long to write about?

One crucial piece of advice: Know your target audience and ensure that what you share is valuable information that will resonate deeply with them. Seize your pen with determination and begin to inscribe on your canvas.

The best way to launch this journey as an author is to meticulously craft an outline for your book or manuscript. Laying out a strategic plan that propels you toward the future you envision is also key to succeeding as an author.

The other part of this is having the relentless patience to write on your own or the determination to find a ghostwriter. Will you, with unwavering resolve, sit down and endure the grueling process of writing yourself? With determination and without distraction, you could write your book in one night.

 The typical timeline to craft a book span from one month to six months—though some blaze through quicker. Some grapple with longhand, pouring their souls onto the page, while others dash through with shorthand, every stroke a battle.

Some authors write feverishly to finish, and before they complete one manuscript, another one is bubbling inside of them. Once they are done, they charge forward to the next project, driven by an insatiable hunger to conquer their creative agenda.

Vocabulary and Definitions:

1.**bio:** [ˈbīō] *noun*

    1. a biography or short biographical profile of someone: "the latest in a series of unauthorized bios"

2. **character:** [ˈker(ə)ktər] *noun*

    1. the mental and moral qualities distinctive to an individual: "running away was not in keeping with her character.

3. **copyright:** [ˈkäpēˌrīt] *noun*

    the exclusive legal right, given to an originator or an assignee to print, publish, perform, film, or record literary, artistic, or musical material, and to authorize others to do the same:
"he issued a writ for breach of copyright" · "works whose copyrights had lapsed."

4. **edit:** (ĕd′ĭt) *verb*

    tr.v. **edited, editing, edits.**

    1. **a.** To prepare (written material) for publication or presentation, as by correcting, revising, or adapting.
        b. To prepare an edition for publication: *edit a collection of short stories.*
        c. To modify or adapt to make it suitable or acceptable: *edited her remarks for a presentation to a younger audience.*

    2. **To** supervise the publication of (a newspaper or magazine, for example).

    3. **To** assemble the components of (a film or soundtrack, for example), as by cutting and splicing.

    4. **To** eliminate; delete: *edited the best scene out.*

5. **format:** [ˈfôrˌmat] *verb*

   formatting *(present participle)*

   1. (especially in computing) arrange or put into a
       format:
       "how to format a document."

6. **foreword:** [ˈfôrˌwərd] *noun*

   a brief introduction to a book, typically by a person other
   than the author:
   "he was kind enough to write a foreword for a book that I
   put out."

7. **ISBN:** [ˌīˌesˌbēˈen] *abbreviation*

   international standard book number, a ten-digit number
   assigned to every book before publication, recording such
   details as language, provenance, and publisher.

   1. An ISBN, or International Standard Book Number, is
       a 13-digit unique identifier assigned to every
       published book. It functions like a fingerprint for a
       book, ensuring that each one can be identified easily
       and accurately anywhere in the world.
   2. Whether you are buying a book online, checking it
       out at a library, or searching for it in a bookstore, the
       ISBN is what allows you to locate that specific title
       among millions of others.

8. **manuscript:** [ˈmanyəˌskrip(t)] noun

>   a book, document, or piece of music handwritten rather
>   than typed or printed:
>   "an illuminated manuscript."

9. **paragraph:** ˈper-ə-ˌgraf ˈpa-rə-

>   **1.** a: A section of writing, consisting of one or more sentences,
>   focusing on a single point or speaker, starting on a new, usually
>   indent line. Example: The editor wrote the introductory
>   paragraphs.
>
>   b: A brief composition or note complete in one paragraph.

10. **synopsis**: [səˈnäpsəs] *noun*

>   *synopsis (noun) synopses (plural noun)*

>   **1.** a summary or general survey of something:
>   "a synopsis of the accident"
>   - an outline of the plot of a book, play, movie,
>   or episode of a television show.

The summary should include the most important plot points and
characters. Your summary should get the main point of the book
across to someone who has never read the actual book.

11.**title page:** [ˈtīdəl ˌpāj] *noun*

>   a page at the beginning of a book giving its title, the names
>   of the author and publisher, and other publication
>   information.

Writing Genres:

Action	Entertainment	Legal	Reviewing
Adventure	Environment	Medical	Romance
Activity	Erotica	Melodrama	Love
Adult	Experience	Men's	Satire
Advice	Family	Military	Sci-fi
Animal	Fan fiction	Music	Scientific
Arts	Fantasy	Mystery	Self Help
Biographical	Fashion	Mythology	Spiritual
Business	Finance	Nature	Sports
Career	Folklore	News	Supernatural
Children's	Food/Cooking	Nonsense	Technology
Comedy	Foreign	Opinion	Teen
Community	Genealogy	Parenting	Thriller/Suspense
Computers	Ghost	Personal	Tragedy
Contest	Health	Pets	Transportation
Contest Entry	History	Philosophy	Travel
Crime/Gangster	Hobby/Craft	Political	Tribute
Cultural	Holiday	Psychology	War
Dark	Home/Garden	Reference	Western
Death	Horror/Scary	Regional	Women's
Detective	How-To	Relationship	Writing
Drama	Inspirational	Religious	Young Adult
Educational	Internet/Web	Research	
Emotional			

Writing Prompts:

1) Write about an abstract painting that you have seen this year. Write five to ten sentences.

_____

_____

_____

_____

_____

_____

_____

_____

_____

_____

2) What was the funniest thing you ever saw? Write it in the form of a poem.

_____

_____

_____

_____

_____

_____

3) Imagine a jungle with ten different animals in it. Examples: elephants, monkeys, cheetahs, and birds etc. Now write a short story about one of the animals as the character.

_____

_____

_____

_____

_____

_____

4) Write about your favorite poet and explain why they are your favorite.

_____

_____

_____

_____

_____

_____

5) Rewrite the fairy tale ending to the "Three Little Pigs" that would make people think.

_____

_____

_____

_____

_____

_____

6) Create an advertisement to sell one of your favorite toys or games. Write a post about the games or toys you would like to sell.

_____

_____

_____

_____

_____

_____

7) Imagine you are a genie in a bottle that drifted onto a seashore. And you could not get out until your birthday? What would you do? Write about this experience and how you feel.

_____

_____

_____

_____

_____

_____

8) Create an article with the word "Stop" and it is the title and first sentence of the article.

_____

_____

_____

_____

_____

_____

9) If someone would give you $1000.00 today, what would you buy and why? Draft a short story about your encounter.

_____

_____

_____

_____

_____

_____

10) What is your favorite holiday of the year and why?

_____

_____

_____

_____

_____

_____

<u>The 100 Most Commonly Misspelled Words</u>

The following represents the one hundred most misspelled words, arranged in alphabetical order. It is interesting that half a century later these same words are still causing problems for writers.

Again	From	Something
All right	Getting	Sometimes
Always	Going	Started
An	Happening	Stopped
And	Hear	Surprise
Animals	Heard	Swimming
Another	Here	Than
Around	Him	That's
Asked	Interesting	Their
Babies	Its	Then
Beautiful	Jumped	There
Because	Knew	They
Before	Know	They're
Believe	Let's	Things
Bought	Like	Thought
Came	Little	Threw
Caught	Looked	Through
Children	Many	To
Clothes	Money	Together
Coming	Morning	Too
Course	Mother	Tried
Cousin	Name	Two
Decided	Off	Wanted
Didn't	Once	Went
Different	Our	Were
Dropped	People	With
Every	Pretty	Woman
February	Received	Would
First	Running	Until
For	Said	Very
Friend	School	Yo
Frightened	Some	

<u>Author's Final Words:</u>

I Got Something to Say! The Book in Me"

Have you ever felt that the fire of your life's trials and tribulations could light the way for someone else? Has a divine message been etched into your soul, and begging to be shared with the world? Do you have a voice that aches to be heard but are unsure of how to unleash it?

Enough waiting, it is time to release it and transform that whisper of an idea into a roaring reality. In "I Got Something to Say! The Book in Me" readers will find that it is not just a writer's guide; it is a roadmap to your future. It will ignite your spirit, train your mind, and help you grasp the purpose behind every experience that you have ever endured. You can conquer this! Let us dive into the journey today.

About the Author:

About the Author: Valerie Devone-Grimes comes with this powerful guide on writing to help foster the writing process for authors. She is not just sharing a process; she is unleashing a lifeline for many to grab hold of. This book is your key to unlocking your thoughts and tapping into the gifts within you. She has written over fifty-two books to her credit and looks forward to writing more. Valerie resides in the heart of New York City and is happily married for twenty-eight years and has one beloved son.

The End

Mail Order Form

We are thrilled that you have chosen to read "I Got Something to Say! "The Book in Me": For those interested in exploring additional titles in our collection, these books are available in Spanish and Bangla translations.

Do not forget to stay up to date with our latest publications by following us on Valerie Stories Facebook page.

www.eatnenjoy21.com.

Follow us on Facebook: Eat-n-Enjoy page.

Follow us on Instagram: Eatnenjoy21 page.

https://www.etsy.com/shop/KidsAndKidBooks

We have in stock ABCs Board 26 letters, and Number Board 1-30 for children's education purposes.

Title: (Spanish) La Gran Pesca del Dia \ The Big Catch of the Day

Title: The Adventures of Sheila, The Spotted Pig

Title: New York City Children Short Stories and Workbook

Title: Dad & Me Coloring & Activity Book

Title: Workbook for Kids of all Ages (Sight Words, Colors and Shapes)

Title: Mermaid World Coloring & Activity Book

Title: Mom & Me Coloring & Activity Book for Kids

Title: Unicorn Land Coloring & Activity Book

Title: Letter and Number Tracing Handwriting Practice for Kids

Title: Love From My Little Pals Coloring and Activity Book

Title: Love From My Little Pals Book

Title: Word Search for Kids (Puzzles & Games)

Title: Out of Abundance of the Heart the Mouth Speaks (Poetry)

Title: Moments (Poetry)

Title: Delightful Treats Cookbook

Title: 5 Festive Dinners / Short Cookbook

Title: Toss it up (Salad Book)

Title: Chicken & Meatloaf Lover Classic Dishes Cookbook

Title: Quick Homemade Ideas Cookbook

Title: Grits Fever Cookbook

Title: Gyro & Salad Cookbook

Title: Quick Side Dishes Cookbook

Title: The Power of the Spoken Word

Title: The Spirit of Rejection

Title: How to Have a Prayer Life

Title: Stop Making Excuses

Title: Easy and Relaxation Grown Folk Puzzles for Adults
150+ Puzzles

Title: Challenge Your Mind Puzzle Book for Adults
150+Puzzles

Title: Crossword Puzzles Book for Adults & Seniors #1 & #2

Title: **Misty/ Novella / Fiction:** Her village was destroyed, but she barely escaped. After witnessing her best friend's death, she fled to her hut. She lost her parents and had to start over. Her journey began in college, arriving with a suitcase of rags from Ghana, with her aunt's help, to America.

 She met her roommate, Carol, and faced surprises along the way. While dealing with therapy for her loss, she met Johnatan at the college cafe. Despite everything, she maintained a 4.0 GPA each semester for four years. Her life is set to change dramatically.

Title: **Stuff Happens! / Relationship / Romance:**
Life is full of surprises, especially when it comes to matters of the heart.

Title: **The Street Girl #1 / Relationship / Romance:**
From the streets to unexpected love, these tales will take you on a wild ride.

 Title: **The Keys to my Heart / Novella / Fiction:**
When your spouse means everything to you, and he is not here anymore. What is a girl to do now without her protector? As each day goes by, my heart bleeds for him.

Title: **Broken Promises / Novella / Fiction:**

"Love shattered, a family torn apart. Can the wounds of the past heal, or will the cycle of pain continue?" The struggle is real, and the desire for success consumes me. I can almost taste it on my tongue—the sweet victory of overcoming challenging times and devastating moments.

Total Number of Books_____Shipping & tax_____

Total amount of money_____

Send check or money order along with order form below.

Mail to:

Mrs. Valerie D. Grimes
135-05 Foch Blvd
South Ozone Park, Queens
NY 11420

Client Satisfaction is our priority.
Thank you for all your support.

Please note: All books will be ship when payment received. Allow three weeks for delivery.

Name_____

Address_____

City_____

State_____

Zip_____

Notes

www.ingramcontent.com/pod-product-compliance
Lightning Source LLC
Chambersburg PA
CBHW070944120626
46546CB00004B/1554